Gallery of

Life Lessons

**Every educational journey for both
Student and "Teacher" should be filled
With Life Lesson pit-stops.**

**Richard M. Savona CPA, MBA
& Adjunct Professor**

**Illustrated by Richard M. Savona
(Of course)**

Introduction

"Life imitates art far more than art imitates life" – Oscar Wilde. It was 1889 when Oscar penned this famous quote. Essentially, it means that people do not appreciate the finer aspects of life until the artists have painted it and the poets have written about it.

Well that is what I have set out to do. Contained in my first book are my most treasured Life Lessons that I teach to graduate students at a Delaware University.

These are the exact "primitive" drawings I sketch out on the blackboard and smart-board. It gets their attention. I give them a few minutes to figure it out. Once they have heard and seen their first Life Lesson, they are eager for more.

This book is first dedicated to and targeted at Graduate & Undergraduate Students & Teachers. However, if you are a STUDENT of any age or a "TEACHER" of any subject, you should find great pearls of wisdom to explore and share.

Managers – you are included in this group too! One of your key responsibilities is to teach, inspire and encourage (I call this the TIE concept) your workforce.

So go – imitate the ART the contained in this book. Stir and release the potential within you and the folks around you.

How to Read This Book

You will first notice my artwork. I call it my Life Art. These are the actual pictures I draw in class for my graduate students. Behind each piece of art is a lesson, a Life Lesson. Over the past two years, I have come to the conclusion that my students really enjoy my primitive artwork and the Life Lesson behind it.

My students can tell when I am about to reveal a Life Lesson to them. They see a physical / chemical change in my body demeanor, body gestures and voice. They know they are about to receive a "priceless pearl' of wisdom from another human who has generally traveled more miles than them. Most importantly, they know my true passion – I care about them, their success, their dreams and their current challenges. Several of my students have written me very kind, warm and thoughtful recommendations on my LinkedIn Profile letting me know how I have touched their lives in small and big ways.

When you see a new piece of Life Art, I would like you to reflect, pause and shift into neutral. *Think of yourself in an art gallery.* There is something very special that happens to the human soul when they are reflecting, I mean deeply reflecting, on the original creation from another human being. It is said that each of us has been made in the image and likeness of God. If that is the case, then we have the incredible power to "create" just like our universal Creator. One of the greatest gifts we can give people who "create" things in our lives -- is the moment to reflect, validate, appreciate, and enjoy their creation.

Now – you may not need to deeply reflect too long on some pieces of Life Art. That is OK. After you have digested the Life Lesson, go back to my primitive art and just try to make a mental connection. The greatest gift I can give my readers is the ability to remember and pass along the same (or similar) pearls of inspiration, motivation and guidance. Most of my students, I find, take a minute or two, and replicate my primitive artwork into their notebooks. Especially, if I tell them that my Life Lesson is on the final.☺

One last caveat: I have three students introduce my Life Art to you. I ask them for their initial reactions to the picture. These are three actual students that I had in my Managerial Finance class. However, their individual comments are not from them directly. Rather they reflect the warm, witty and incredibly smart (and sometimes sassy) personalities that emerged in my class. By the end of the book, you should be able to form an interesting opinion for each of them. For me, this is perhaps one of the greatest reasons why I teach in the classroom – to meet and get to know the future leaders of this planet.

How Big is My Target Audience?

So, just how many "students" and "teachers" do we have in the US? It all comes down to how you define STUDENT and TEACHER. In this book, STUDENT is meant to represent all the college and university students, at any point in time. TEACHER is defined as anyone who has a real (and expected) responsibility to formally and informally teach another human being.

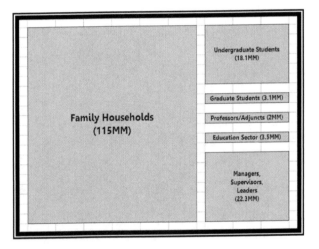

The data above either has been taken from the National Center of Education Statistics (NCES), US Census Bureau or estimated using publicly available information. MM = millions.

Overall, there are approximately 160 million "students" and "teachers" in the US who could benefit from reading, leveraging and applying the Life Lessons in this book. Perhaps just as important is acknowledging that a "primitive piece of art" can be very effective at engaging and drawing in (pun intended ☺) your student audience.

My graduate students know that when I pick up a piece of chalk or marker, I am about to unfold a worthy life lesson – that highlights my passion for teaching, caring and encouragement.

> **If you want to learn how to "hook" your students, put down the fishing rod and pick up the chalk/marker.**
>
> **Create your own Life Lessons Gallery!**

Dedication

This is a fun page in any book. I am sure most authors savor this page because it means that the creation process of writing the book, the pouring out of one's soul -- is complete. So I would like to dedicate this book to people and events in my life who directly/indirectly helped me through this creative process.

#1 - Happy Accidents. First, let me say that it is much easier to write your 2nd book than your first book. While my first book unfortunately has not been published yet, due to licensing issues, the creation and innovation process for this book was much more fun and enlightening. So my first dedication goes to "happy accidents" in life. My frustrations and lessons learned from book #1 fueled tremendous energy for book #2.

#2 – My Soulmate. Second dedication absolutely goes to my wife and soul-mate for 34 years. Mary has been my rock and best friend for most of my life. Everything I have achieved in life has traces of Mary's love and support.

#3 – The Fantastic Four. The Fantastic Four are my children – Tiffany, Ricky, Amanda and Michael. Each of them has truly inspired me with their love and excitement of learning.

#4 – My Amazing (Adopted) Jewish Mother. Next up is Wendy Strawhacker. For the past three years, Wendy has known that my 2nd literary work was bottled up somewhere in my soul. She knew I would eventually give birth. She just didn't know to what. Thank you Wendy for your amazing pearls of wisdom and herculean encouragement. There is something to be said of the love and support of a Jewish mom!

#5 – My New Publishing Friend. I would like to acknowledge my new friend, Harry Fisher, another Adjunct Professor. We met each other in the Faculty Break Room and found out that we share similar passions – teaching and writing books. Harry's inspiration and guidance were exactly what I needed to publish my second literary work. Thank you Harry.

#6 – My Shining Example of "Semper Fi." My Dad has been an amazing source of quiet strength and selflessness for 82 years. He is currently battling prostate cancer with the loving support and day-to-day caretaking from my sister, Jeanne. He enjoys looking back in the rearview mirror much more than looking ahead these days. Just recently, he shared some wonderful stories of when he was a Marine in the Korean War. He corrects me – he "is" still a Marine and very proud of their values and contributions. My Dad has always been, and always will be – my shining example of Semper Fi, which is the Marines motto. It is short for Semper Fidelis which means "always faithful." Thanks Dad for bringing to life this wonderful credo. It is the same value I bring into every classroom, to every student. I promise to continue your amazing legacy of "Semper Fi."

#7 – My Mother, the Dreamer. My Mom was the one person in life who inspired me to dream big. She made sure I went to the best (affordable) schools growing up. While she wanted me to be a doctor and treat people's physical ailments, it turns out, I am not too far off course. It is a little bit of a stretch but instead of touching lives on the medical side, I am touching lives on the academic side. The doctor teaches, inspires and educates the patient on a physical level while the teacher / professor teaches, inspires and educates on the academic/motivational level. My Mom would have thoroughly enjoyed this book. However, she passed away 5 years ago on June 30, 2010. She bravely battled multiple myeloma. So Mom, I know where you are – and I do not believe you need to rely on Amazon's distribution network to enjoy this book and dedication. Thank you for helping me dream big!

#8 – The Ultimate Creative Source. While I was doing some research for this book, I stumbled upon the 12 Universal Laws. They are things like: (1) Law of Divine Oneness, (2) Law of Action, (3) Law of Attraction, (4) Law of Polarity, and (5) Law of Cause and Effect. Then there are additional physical laws such as (1) Biogenesis, (2) Chemistry, (3) Planetary Motion, (4) Physics, and (5) Mathematics. These laws were created by a God who wants us to "create" our own destiny, lives, happiness and joy. The only way we can do this in a sustaining way is to have laws of the universe govern our creation process.

I carried the "seed" of this book for two years. Then my new friend Harry asked me this one question, "Do you have a book that you want to publish." I said yes and no. I told him I had this idea but had not started the writing process. He said, "Just start." One week later, I had completed 95% of the manuscript. That kind of creative energy only comes from the Creative Source. So I would like to make my final dedication to the Ultimate Creative Source of the Universe. Thank you Lord for our desire and passion to create as well as our ability to fully enjoy the creative process and its outcomes (including primitive artwork).

About the Author

Rich Savona is an Adjunct Professor at a Delaware University. He is a CPA with his MBA in Finance. He has over 30 years of financial, accounting and project management experience in the banking, healthcare, and small startup industries.

Rich looks forward to speaker engagement opportunities for graduate students, undergraduate students and the professor community to discuss and reinforce the Life Lessons contained in this book.

Touring the Life Lessons Gallery

Let Me Introduce to You 3 Special Graduate Students...

Throughout the book, you will get to know three graduate students who were in my Managerial Finance class. While their comments and "art interpretations" are not their observations directly, I try to capture the essence and spirit of their personalities. You know the "inner fire" on what makes people tick and determines how people view the world.

Victoria – is a young Asian woman who is incredibly smart and driven. When I first met Victoria in class, she was quiet and reserved. Not quiet in a shy way. Quiet in a strong way. During class introductions, we find that she comes from a highly educated family. She has already achieved one master's degree with an undergrad degree in bio-engineering. On some days, she has dreams of becoming a doctor. After all, her father was only a neuroscience doctor who specialized in research. On other days, a free spirit emerges who wants to explore more of the business world.

During the course, the class and I discover that she has a strong foundation in math and is extremely comfortable with finance calculations such as Net Present Value (NPV), Internal Rate of Return (IRR), and Weighted Avg Cost of Capital, otherwise known as the WACC. My students love the "wacc."

Since 10% of the each students grade is based on their collaboration, engagement and active thought leadership with the class, students are looking for opportunities to share and support. Amazing things happen when the incentives are structured carefully.

Well by week 4, Victoria is teaching, coaching, tutoring about half the class. Everyone in the class is comfortable with her and truly appreciate her passion for learning and conquering new subject material. And what emerges throughout the 7 week course, is a very self confident, marginally sassy attitude that works for everyone. So I would categorize Victoria's observations and personality as: CARING and SASSY.

Michael, on the other hand, is a 26 year old engineering student. His undergraduate degree is in civil engineering. He is pursuing his MBA. Michael is quiet and reserved and very much the intellectual type. When he asks questions, they are deep, critical thinking questions.

Very quickly, I tap Michael to be one of the class Ambassadors. People quickly "tackle" him and ask for his assistance. His demeanor is gentle and he never refuses to help a fellow classmate.

Michael has a very dry sense of humor. You know the kind of humor that generally belongs to the high intellect folks. Many of his observations of the Life Art will come from his engineering slant and his extremely good, but dry, sense of humor. So, I would categorize Michael's observations and personality as: INTELLECTUAL and WITTY.

Then we have David. David is a little bit older than Victoria and Michael. I would guess in his mid-thirties. He is an Italian and his warmth comes through immediately when he does his life introduction to the class. He mentions that his passion is art and drawing. He goes onto say that music runs deep in his family. I find out that his dad is a musician and a drummer – no less! I start kidding around with David that I need to meet and jam with his dad. He chuckles.

What I loved about David was that he sat in class each week with an impish, slightly devilish kind of smile. And I love when my students give me those kinds of observable queues. Because part of my job as a teacher is to bring out the best (and enjoyable) qualities of each student.

So when I see that particular smile surface on David's face, I call on him. And I ask him to share with the class what is on his mind. Initially, as he shares his thoughts, it may seem a bit cynical, but as he goes on to explain, he generally backs up his opinions with life experiences. So I would categorize David's observations and personality as: CREATIVE and PLAYFUL.

One last reminder about why other's views are so important. Let's revisit the gallery analogy. Most people generally go to the art gallery with friends. Once inside, people put on their "contemplative / reflective" hats. One by one, people stand in front of the artwork, look, think, reflect and contemplate. At this moment in time, they have formed an initial opinion. Now, undoubtedly, the next question that is uttered by someone in that party is, "So what do you think?"

Stop and think about where we are. Why are we so hungry for other people's opinion and insight when we are in an art gallery? Because I believe the human soul desperately does not want to miss something that they could have seen, appreciated, and marveled at.

Artwork, a small piece of creation, has a way of connecting with the soul and offers us an opportunity to "pause and reflect." So, I am trying my very best to perhaps replicate the process of being in an art gallery with a party of people, appreciating and reflecting on unique pieces of Life-Art that I have created for my graduate students. The people in your party happen to be Victoria, Michael and David. Thoroughly enjoy their company. I know I did.

What do you see?

Victoria: Hmm. This is a hard one. Looks like the planet earth about to swallow up the moon.

Michael: It reminds me of perhaps an atom with the nucleus being the larger circle and the smaller circle being the electron.

David: As a kid, I loved bubbles. It kind of reminds me of bubbles where the big one looks like it is ready to pop.

The Larger Circle.

This is one of my favorite Life Lessons and perhaps one of the first that I created in graduate class. Specifically this Life Lesson was created in Managerial Finance. Part Finance and part Accounting, this course was required to be taken by all non-MBA graduates. These students have not been exposed to any Finance or Accounting.

Can you guess what the smaller circle represents? In every class, with a few helpful hints, I always have one student that nails it.   It represents ALL the accumulated knowledge, experience, and wisdom that ONE person has gained in their life (to-date).

Now can you guess what the larger circle is? Yes – it represents ALL the accumulated knowledge, experience and wisdom that 8 billion people on the planet have aggregated. To keep it more realistic and personal, the Larger Circle is all the rest of the students in the class. Oops – we forgot one person. The teacher. So it represents all other students + the teacher.

Why do I discuss this life lesson, in Week 1 of the new course? It generally happens around 6:30 pm – one hour into the new class. This is the part of the syllabus where my students find out that 10% of their final grade comes from the evaluation and assessment of their classmates. What is being evaluated is the "quality and quantity" of the thought leadership demonstrated in class and online in their discussion board.

Some students naturally ask me how this evaluation process works. I go on to explain. Students have 100 points to allocate to the entire class, including themselves. At the end of the course, Week 7, the students submit to me their assessment forms. Let's say that I have 15 students in my class. 100 points divided by 15 people = 6.7 points.

I further explain to my students that there are 2 groups that emerge. One group of students is the "happy, non-confrontational" group. They basically give all the students the same score. Then there is the "fair, management thinking" group. These people have no problem giving another student a 0 if they have not contributed online or in class.

Students never see their scores from other students. The results are given to me and kept confidential. Once students realize that I am encouraging people to support and share, and expecting that people support and share, they get more comfortable with the 2 circles.

I now start to share real-life business stories. I explain that the people who move to the top of the company ladder are able to tap the Larger Circle with ease and comfort. They know who to go to, who to trust, and who has the credible opinions in the organization. These leaders realize they do not have to possess the knowledge and solution (to the next big problem). All they have to do is to be able to utilize this intangible asset (the collective intellectual property) of the organization with lightning speed.

I go on to tell my students that one of the reasons that they are going to graduate school is to force themselves out of their comfort zones, learn to respect and value the opinions of others, and to get proficient at learning how to tap the Larger Circle. I emphasize that if they can learn this in my class, they will successfully do this in the workforce.

I am happy to report that at least half of my students totally embrace this new opportunity, this new expectation. They become "enriched" and empowered to share, support, teach, inspire and motivate other students who are struggling with this new material. At this point, when I see this "chemical change" happening in my classroom, I smile because I realize that the enrichment process (that I started) is now producing "fission" and releasing the "mini-teachers" in my classroom. You can't have a bad day when you see that happen before your eyes!

Reflection Point ... in the Life Art Gallery

Please go back to the Life Art picture and now reflect on the small circle and the Larger Circle. These circles should take on new meanings now.

If you are a teacher, it will never happen (or happen in insignificant doses) without creating a linkage to their final grade. Oh – you need more proof? Sure. Let me give you my first experience teaching (Cost Accounting) to 12 students at night.

As a CPA for more than 30 years, I know that this stuff (Accounting) is very hard to learn. Why? Well because you are essentially learning a new language + a new science. That's what makes it so challenging for many students. But I recognize this so that I create a grade incentive to read the chapter material before coming to class. Say what? I give them a chapter quiz in class. 10 simple questions. It took them 10 minutes to complete. It allowed me to rapidly build their knowledge if they had plowed through the material once out of class.

About midway through the course, I had one student ask me if we could forego the chapter quiz at the beginning of the class. I thought about it. The average age of my students in that class was mid-30's. So I agreed under one condition – that they continue reading the chapter materials before class. They all agreed. The next week I start reviewing the new chapter material. What do you think I discovered? Not one student, not one, read the chapter before class. The following week, we all returned to taking a 10-question chapter quiz at the beginning of class.

As teachers, we must never forget that we must create a learning environment that encourages students to do the right thing, even though it requires more work. As I tell each of my students before they complete my course, my goal is not to receive a Christmas card from them in the current year. My goal is to receive a card from them 5 years from now when they have had ample time to leverage, build and apply this finance and accounting knowledge and get promoted along the way.

Let me share an important reflection point for Supervisors, Managers, Directors and Executives. I spent over 25 years in the financial services industry. That means I received about 50 semi-annual and annual performance reviews. Guess what? People only pay attention to what they are financially incented to do. All the soft stuff, like working together effectively, supporting each other, and improving collaboration and innovation skills – they get thrown out the window.

Why do managers forget that they are leading and managing the equivalent of a huge ship? The only way that the ship will reach its destination on time is if ALL the rowers have their oars in the water, at the same time, and rowing with the same speed and intensity. If rowers become out of sync for a few seconds, it will be felt immediately. So, as a manager, take the road less traveled. Explain to your department that you expect them to share, support, teach, help, inspire and motivate each other. It would be very easy to formalize the same process I use in my class on a quarterly basis. Just explain that each employee gets 100 points to allocate to all their co-workers. You will get great data and so will they. And since they will be receiving it quarterly, they will have ample time to adjust and correct their current workplace behaviors to rise in the ratings. At the end of the day, why would you want to promote someone other than the top supporter / nurturer / motivator?

What do you see?

Victoria: I know this one. It is a picture of a man in the future with the i-chip installed in his head. You know, it's coming. You would be amazed at all the bioengineering innovations that will ultimately be implanted in the human body.

Michael: Maybe it is supposed to represent a portal of knowledge into the man's head.

David: You guys are overthinking this one. I think it is one of those moles from Austin Power that we are not supposed to stare at or even mention. Mole. Mole. Mole. Boy that feels good.

The Power of One Thought.

We have all heard this one before. The power of positive thinking. However, more and more research is being conducted on the "power of thoughts." I recently had an opportunity to see the documentary movie, The Secret. The movie focuses on the Law of Attraction.

Up until this movie, I had never heard about this Law of Attraction. Essentially, the overall theme of the movie is about how people "attract into their life" -- what they focus on, what they think about, what they fret about. OK – now let's dig a little deeper.

The movie features a number of leading philosophers, healers and even quantum physicists! Yes quantum physicists. Both the scientific community and the philosophical community are converging on an astounding revelation that our thoughts – which have specific frequencies and vibrations -- essentially "attract" into our lives what we are focusing on.

Of course there are skeptics out there. There has to be a lot of them. Because that is one of the reasons why the Law of Attraction is still dubbed – The Secret. Either people have not heard of it or they choose not to believe in it.

One of the people interviewed in the movie is Bob Proctor, a philosopher. He makes a very compelling comparison of the Law of Attraction to electricity. Think about electricity. Do we really understand how it works? Not really. Yet we all enjoy its benefits. We also know that if used properly, it can cook a man's meal. If not used properly, it can cook a man! That is a great parallel analogy for the Law of Attraction. Like electricity, it is always working, always on. Like electricity, we can either channel its energy or not.

So how does this apply to the graduate student? It is amazing what kinds of thoughts my students bring into my class. "I can't do this. It's too hard. There is too much material. I don't have enough time in my schedule. I never had Finance or Accounting in undergrad school. I hate numbers. No, I am sorry, I loathe numbers. This stuff does not make sense. Why does a Balance Sheet have to balance?" You get the point.

So if I am going to be a positive force in the lives of my graduate students, I must take on this challenge like a philosopher and quantum physicist would. When I talk about this Life Lesson, I tell my students that when I hear them utter a "negative thought" that I will address it and help them overcome that negative feeling. The movie (The Secret) goes on to explain that the power is in the feelings produced by the thought, not the thought itself. The "feelings" have the emotional energy that is released into the universe, where they start to attract those resources needed to fulfill your feeling – whether it is positive or negative.

If the class shows interest in this Life Lesson, I go on to share with them an experiment that was conducted many years ago on the subject of thinking/believing. One group of people (say a 100) were brought into a room and given a jar with a lid on it. This group was told that the jar was screwed on very, very tight.

The scientists who were conducting the experiment then told the group that they only expected a handful of people (out of 100) to unscrew the jar lid. When the group was told to proceed, less than 10 opened the jars.

Another group of people (another 100) were brought into another room and given the same jars. However, this time, the scientists conducting the experiment told them that the lid was screwed on with minimal effort. In fact, they told the group they were expecting about 80 people to unseat the lid. They were told to proceed. About 90 people successfully unscrewed the lid.

Here is what that experiment shows us – we believe what we are told. It doesn't matter if someone else is doing the talking or you are doing the talking (internally). By the way – all 200 jars were screwed on with the same amount of effort.

Henry Ford once uttered, *"Whether you believe you can, or believe you can't – you are right."* Wow. Imagine truly unlocking the power behind that statement. So likewise, aren't graduate students going to school to partially/fully unlock the mysteries of the universe that govern us, our success, and our future?

One of my students raises a question – how does this really apply in the classroom. So I quickly create an experiment in class. I ask one student to come up to the front of the class and say only negative things about my course, its difficulty, the workload, and the fact that they are getting nothing out of it. Then I ask them to sit down.

I ask another student to come to the front of the class and do the exact opposite. I ask them to comment on how excited they are to be taking the course, how they will apply it tremendously on their job, how they are working hard, but still experiencing some difficulties understanding several topics. Then I ask them to sit down.

I now ask the class to vote on which student they would rather help. I collect the votes. It is unanimous. No one wants to help the negative student. Everyone wants to help the positive student. There is a moment of silence and reflection in the room. They now see how they either "attract in" or "repel out" resources in life that could have been available to them. What is even more revealing is that several students commented that they were ready to call the positive student and ask them if they needed help --- even if the explicit request for help was not made.

Reflection Point ... in the Life Art Gallery

Doesn't matter who you are. Student, teacher, parent, manager or executive. Go 30-60 days only thinking positive, grateful thoughts and eliminate all the "negative chatter" that we all battle with. Just watch how much joy/happiness you attract into your life. Including that A if you are graduate student ☺

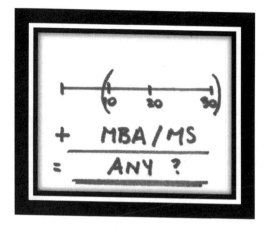

What do you see?

Victoria: Uh oh. We have got a few formulas here and you know how I love formulas and math.

Michael: Looks like we are supposed to be adding some kind of timeline with an MBA or MS degree.

David: Michael, pretty good. But I am really stumped on what it equals. Any – what?

Enriching Uranium & the Graduate Student.

This is probably one of the first Life Lesson pieces of art that I used in my graduate classes about 2 years ago. Perhaps it was my 2nd graduate class I was teaching. And it (the pearl) came out of nowhere. As I recall, it was in response to something a student said that was very limiting in how they really viewed their master's degree.

Can you guess what the artwork is trying to convey? The timeline is the number of years a person has accumulated in the business world. The MBA / MS is obvious. It is the additional component of a person's body of knowledge. The ANY represents any problem that needs to be solved in business.

So the Life Lesson that I teach passionately to my graduate students is this – that once they have acquired 10 years of business experience and their completed master's degree - that they should be able to handle ANY business problem dropped in their lap.

When I share this with my students, a number of them are puzzled. Perhaps you are too. Good – that means that there is a learning opportunity right around the corner for you. But it's time for a good story.

One of my favorite authors is Malcolm Gladwell. He is the author of books like The Tipping Point, Blink, Outliers and What the Dog Saw. They are good reads because he has a way of unraveling every day mysteries – such as why is February the big birthday month for hockey players and how did NYC successfully eliminate graffiti from most of their trains in the 1990s. He "peels the onion" and offers social, psychological, philosophical reasons why certain things happen or exist. There is one particular story I like that he does on the Beatles.

Many people will undoubtedly argue that the Beatles were perhaps the best band of all times. I am a musician and would not argue with that statement. Now most of those people would attribute qualities like musical geniuses, the most creative, and most gifted musicians of our times – to the Beatles and their success. However, Malcolm Gladwell pulls the thread here and uncovers a more likely reason for their success in America.

Before the Beatles landed in America back in 1964, they were playing the club circuit in England and Germany. All the Beatles were in bands before they joined forces, but came together when they were still very young. Once their lineup was established with Ringo Starr as their drummer, they were ready to takeoff. But not so quickly. Their manager started booking them at gigs where they played for 10-12 hours continuously. And they did this a lot. While they may have gone home with blisters on their fingers every night, they also went home with a deep appreciation of getting to know each other. If you are a musician, you will understand this statement – music is all about chemistry amongst the band.

It turns out that the Beatles had amassed about 10,000 hours playing with each other in the clubs in Europe during the late 1950s and early 1960s. When they landed in America, they were ready to take off because their foundation as a band had been already solidified. They had already achieved great chemistry with each other because of the 10,000 hours they had logged in with each other. Still not sold? Just check out their first campy movie Hard Day's Night. Remember, they are NOT actors.

They are musicians. What the camera caught was a deep affection they had for each other. Every time I watch that movie I always pick up something new.

So now let me leverage the Beatles, 10,000 hours, and the graduate student. If you have been working 10 years that is approximately 20,000 hours in the workplace. Add to that a master's degree. What more do you need? You should be the equivalent of a Beatle in the workplace, right.

I tell my students that if they CANNOT handle any problem after working for 10 years with their completed master's degree, that it is their problem. They let this happen to themselves. So a few students now ask me what they are to do. I passionately tell them that they need a shift in their awareness. If they are not actively learning critical thinking in EVERY graduate class, they are to do their best to request it from the teacher, to the point where they do a "Vulcan mind meld" with their teacher. I finish by telling the students that I should feel like an "empty vegetable" at the end of every class. If I do – that means they have done their part by actively extracting all the critical knowledge out of me for their future use.

One last clarification: when I say that a graduate student with 10 years of business experience + their master's degree should be able to handle "any" problem, this is what I mean. Handle does not mean solve. Handle means to be able to (1) understand the problem; (2) assess the logical impacts on customers and various departments; (3) break down the problem into logical components; and (4) find a subject matter expert (SME) to assist with the potential solutions. That is what I mean when I say – handle ANY problem.

So why did I choose the art title – Enriching uranium and the Graduate Student? It really does not relate to the Life Art picture. OK – let me explain please.

Uranium is the chemical element of atomic number 92, a gray, dense radioactive metal used as a fuel in nuclear reactors. It is one of the heaviest metals found on earth. Additionally, it can be found in several different forms called isotopes. Apparently, the isotope U-235 is the one that is used in nuclear reactors.

In its natural state, there is nothing going on with uranium. It must be "enriched" to unleash its awesome potential. The U-235 isotope has 92 protons and 143 electrons; hence that is why it was named U-235. When the U-235 nucleus is enriched (not quite sure of the enrichment process), and it captures one moving electron, it splits in two (fission) and immediately releases energy in the form of heat. Without the enrichment process, there is no power, no energy. With enrichment, there is tremendous power, tremendous energy, and tremendous potential.

Same thing with a graduate student. Or an undergraduate student. Or a worker ("student") in the workplace. Without the necessary enrichment, there is inert potential. However, once the "teachers" (people responsible for imparting a body of knowledge – in academic world or business world) have provided the necessary environment to capture "interest and excitement" (this is equivalent to the capturing of one moving electron in uranium), energy, power, excitement, dreams, innovation are released. Summed up, when the "teachers" on this planet have done their job, they have released the tremendous potential in the students.

So whether we realize it or not, as teachers, we are in the enrichment business. Just the thought of enriching some other human being on the planet – doesn't that get your creative juices flowing?

Reflection Point ... in the Life Art Gallery

Go back and look at the picture again. If you are close to the "inflection point" (a time of significant change, a turning point) – then all you need to do is to change your thinking, your timeline and expectations. More importantly, you have a responsibility to yourself right now. If you do not know how your company generates revenues completely, find out. If you do not understand the critical operations of your company, go learn them. If you do not know your company's key competitors, shame on you (sorry) – fix that. What are you waiting for? Look at that picture one more time. Your timeline is not infinite. Make an impact now. Think uranium. Think enrichment. Imagine the release of your "inert" potential now.

What do you see?

Victoria: It has a facial appearance. But I am clueless what it is supposed to represent. I see the word soup. I am starting to get hungry. Is Rich going to give us a break soon, or what?

Michael: Looks like this guy is balancing a can of soup on his nose. And maybe they are in a "no juggling" zone.

David: No you guys are way off. It reminds me of that game called concentration. I think it is a puzzle of some sorts that we have to put together. How about it means something like it's not going to be cloudy today?

Eliminating the -- I Can't.

I could not resist. As I was pulling this book together with all my "artwork" – my mind started to flash back to the days of the Concentration Game on TV. You remember, it was the game where contestants would answer a question and piece of the puzzle would be revealed. Once enough pieces were revealed, the phrase could be deciphered.

This should not be too difficult. It is a picture of an "eye," a "can" and a "t." Put them all together and you get the phrase I can't. Now onto the Life Lesson.

This is really like a subchapter from the Power of a Thought. But there is value in focusing on it and discussing it. This is perhaps the most common phrase I hear from all students, applied to many different situations. "I can't do this or that." If you are a graduate student, immediately stop saying these words, especially in front of your professor. If you are a human being, immediately stop saying these words to all the people in your life. What you do not realize is how powerful these words are – when they are said, when they are heard, when they are processed by our brains, and when they are believed by our spirit.

I am currently teaching a McGraw Hill course called Financial Accounting for MBAs. I am now learning and using for the first time their "Connect" product, which is their new educational technology platform. The textbook is digital, the critical content is highlighted in yellow, questions are delivered to the student as they read, and correct and incorrect questions are recorded for continued reinforcement. Like the iPhone, this is cool stuff.

Another neat feature of this new online teaching tool is that it keeps track of every minute spent (by the student) in chapter readings, homework assignment, chapter quizzes, and practice sessions. I can see which students are putting in the time and which ones aren't. Unfortunately, the student can no longer hide with these electronic tools.

As a teacher, it is easy for me to see tight correlations between grades and time invested. In fact, it is very close to a +1.0 correlation – for you statistic fans. But I now share with my students another correlation that might not be so obvious.

I draw a few things on the board and show my students that, like time, attitude is a heavy predictor of grades. I hone in on the "I Can't" response that I hear from several students every class. I further discuss that students who are comfortable using this kind of language are also comfortable accepting complacency in their final grades. It is surprising to find these students willing to accept a C.

I ask my students in the early classes, who wants to receive a C as a final grade. Nobody raises their hands. So I go onto explain that if nobody is intentionally working toward a C, then nobody should be willing to accept the consequences that go along with the "I Can't" language.

You still are not sure that language has that much power to be restricting and self-defeating? For more than 17 years, I worked for a great credit card company in Delaware who achieved legendary success by doing things a little differently. We had motivational quotes painted on the walls. We had motivational sayings above every doorway in the company. We also had words that could never be used in the spoken and written language.

OK – if I have piqued your curiosity, let me share a few examples with you. We were never allowed to use the word "employee" – it was too demeaning. Everyone that worked at the company was a "person / people". You weren't allowed to use the word "training" because only pets were trained. People were educated. And the word customer was so important to our business and culture that it was always capitalized when it referred to the "external Customer."

Reflection Point ... in the Life Art Gallery

If you are a student – any kind of student – part of your educational journey is one of enlightenment. Which means that you need to be open to new ideas, new paradigm shifts, and new ways of looking at the world. Try to go 30 days without using the words I CAN'T. You might even want to keep track with tick marks of the number of times you unconsciously say these words. Immediately, you should see a more positive outlook emerging, especially when you are facing new challenges in your life.

At the risk of repeating myself, let me share this pearl of wisdom again from Henry Ford,
"Think you can, think you can't – you are right."

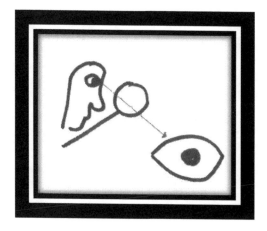

What do you see?

Victoria: Hey, looks like something from the Sci-Fi channel.

Michael: I think it is trying to say something about someone's vision. Perhaps something like X-ray vision.

David: Maybe the object is a mirror and the person is seeing something interesting in his eye. Perhaps the plank in his eye. I know you guys have no idea what that means (smile).

Become a Noticer.

The Noticer by Andy Andrews. One of the best books I have ever come across in my life. Let me share a quick story of how Andy and his book came into my life about 10 years ago.

One day, I was shopping with my wife in one of those discount retail stores and came upon the aisle of books for sale. The entire aisles were books for sale, heavily discounted and piled 10 to 15 books high in some cases. I remember asking myself, "How will

I find anything meaningful in this pile of stuff." I walked up and down the aisle 2-3 times, until I came upon this small pile of books called, The Noticer. There was nothing special about the book cover. In fact, the color of the cover was like a pea-green with a small suitcase in the middle of the cover with the words, The Noticer.

I picked up one copy for my summer vacation reading. Once I started it, I couldn't put it down. I highly recommend the book so I will not go into a lot of details. Essentially, the main character comes into the lives of different people living in a local community and starts to "notice" things about them. It turns out that the simple act of noticing --- where people are in their lives, what their hardships are, and what dreams they had abandoned – starts to re-awaken people. He miraculously brings new hope and encouragement to each of the people – he notices.

After I read the book and returned from vacation, I went back to the discount retail store and purchased another 10 copies. I decided to give each one of my 4 kids their own personalized copy. Additionally, I decided to give a copy to my business partners. Years later, I would find myself giving my "personal copy" to a client executive who was badly treating his employees (300 in total). His worst treatment of all is that he never – noticed anyone. Not in the hallways. Not in the parking lots. Not even in the church pews on Sunday.

OK – now onto my application in the classroom. As a teacher, I was surprised to find that I needed to "actively promote" the idea that students are to "notice" each other to see if anyone needs help, reassurance and support. I remember in particular an older student, in her fifties, who made the comment in class that she was not able to evaluate her classmates on their class participation and participation in the online discussion board. You see, I attach 10 points of a student's final grade to active discussion in class and online.

When I asked her why she could not evaluate her classmates, she said that she didn't know them. What she meant was that she did not take the time to link their names with their faces. So when she looked at the evaluation report of student names, she had no idea who was who.

I immediately responded and said to her, "That is interesting. Because I have been in the same class with you and all these students, and I know their names, and a little bit of their life story (that I was able to pick up from their student bio), completed for the first class.

WOW. Can you imagine grown mature adults, working hard to complete their master's degrees, and they forget or not think it is important to "notice" fellow classmates?

Well – because my teaching philosophy includes TIE (teach, inspire and encourage), I go out of my way and tell people that it is their job to "notice" people in their life. We have all experienced good leaders and bad leaders. The good leaders, despite the chaos and craziness of running a company, have the ability to notice the existence and good work of others.

Still not sold? Let me share one of my first work experiences that I still fondly remember to this day. I was 16 years old and had just gotten my first real job at Burger King, a new store that had just opened in Staten Island, NY in the late 1970s. As I quickly learned all the food stations, Calvin, the general manager, would often bark at me, "Savona can you sweep and mop the floor for me?" To most young people, they would disdain doing something like that. For me, however, since I really liked clean and organization, I didn't mind doing it.

I would always go out of my way to discard the old water in the bucket, use fresh hot water, and include a prescribed batch of some ammonia cleaner. When I finished the floor, it looked spotless. Not one grease streak at all which is an incredible task considering that people are constantly dropping food and french fry grease all the time. I always noticed my good work but I wasn't sure if anyone else did -- until we had our first employee meeting.

Calvin went through a number of things on his agenda. I can't recall any of them until he started talking about the process of cleaning floors. He turned around to about 60 employees and said that whenever they were asked / told to clean the floor – they were to clean the floor – like Savona. Calvin noticed. By the way, I am going back close to 40 years to retell this story for you. People never forget when they have been noticed.

Reflection Point ... in the Life Art Gallery

If you are in the classroom, "notice" your students. Take the time to get to know (notice) their names. Take the time and get to know (notice) what their hobbies and interests are from their class introduction. And don't forget to empower your students and encourage them to notice when fellow classmates are confused and struggling. I teach Financial Accounting and Managerial Finance at the graduate level to students who have never been exposed to those disciplines. So I always have a few students who struggle to get it and keep up. But I notice their struggles in class. And I tell my students (including my Ambassadors) to notice when people need a TIE – teaching, inspiration and encouragement.

Now if you are in the workplace, this small act of "noticing" can reap great, great returns. Look people in the eye. Notice them. When they appear confused or down, notice it and offer some help. Because if you don't the Laws of (1) Cause and Effect, and (2) Attraction will smack you when you least expect it. Let me finish off my client story with this comment from one of the employees: "If I saw John, stranded by the side of the road, broken-down, I would never stop and help him. I would just simply ignore (not notice) him, and smile while driving past him."

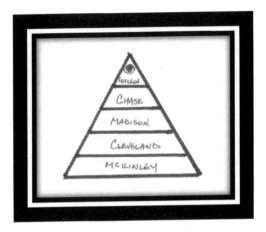

What do you see?

Victoria: I don't have to be an engineer to figure this one out. It obviously is a pyramid. Not sure why those names are in the pyramid.

Michael: The eye at the top somewhat reminds me of the eye on the back of the dollar. Yep. It is the all-seeing eye. Big brother.

David: I think most of the names are US presidents. However, not sure if they appear on any currencies – if the picture is all about money.

What the Egyptians and SMEs Know About Pyramids.

OK – have you guessed it yet? It is Bloom's Taxonomy. Bloom's "pyramid" attempts to identify how the human brain learns something new. The six levels of learning are: (1)

Remembering, (2) Understanding, (3) Applying, (4) Analyzing, (5) Evaluating, and (6) Creating.

Now when I present Bloom's Taxonomy in class, most of my graduate students get bored and start yawning. Understandable. I need to really relate to their lives and why they are going to school. So now I have inserted names of the presidents that either still do or once graced the face of certain currencies as follows:

> $100,000 bill = Woodrow Wilson

> $10,000 bill = Salmon Chase (not a president)

> $5,000 bill = James Madison

> $1,000 bill = Grover Cleveland

> $500 bill = William McKinley

The connection that should be happening now is this – as students advance upward through the pyramid as it relates to the "learning acquisition process" – the more potential money they can generate in their lives.

If we take the life of Steve Jobs and apply Bloom's taxonomy, we see why he was hugely successful in the introduction of devices that have changed the world. Steve Jobs was an expert in the computer and telecommunications market. Most of his time was spent at the very top of the pyramid – CREATING new products and new services based upon an incredibly deep and broad knowledge of the market.

When my students start complaining about the amount of time they are spending outside of the classroom, I remind them that there are no shortcuts to advancing within the pyramid. You only advance once you have acquired and demonstrated a certain level of proficiency (mastery) with the current level.

Real excitement in school and in the business world happens at the James Madison level – you know when you can apply what you have learned.

Reflection Point ... in the Life Art Gallery

As teachers, we must provide ample opportunities for students to apply what they have learned, remembered and understood. Without sufficient application opportunities, learning cannot be effectively reinforced and retained.

As a Manager or Business Leader just realize that employees must be given opportunities to work through the pyramid. Errors are to be expected in early stages of application. So please set expectations accordingly. All too often, we hear of the manager who had a meltdown when an employee made a mistake after she learned something new. If you try to shortcut the application process, the long-term retention process will be compromised.

What do you see?

Victoria: C'mon – can't get any easier – this is a care package.

Michael: Agreed. But that is too easy. It must have a deeper meaning that we need to unlock.

David: Agreed. Wow – this is the first time that we all agreed. However, it looks like one side of the box is about to collapse. Kind of ironic that if it's a care package, it was not packaged with care. Pun intended ☺

Why You Should Be In the Care Package Business.

Trust me, I know what you are thinking. Really – we need a chapter on Care. Yes. Based on my graduate students, the answer is yes. OK let's get into it.

As a professor, I always start with the basic assumption that a student cares about his/her studies because they have "elected" to put themselves through this journey – not to mention, that they have paid lots of dollars to enjoy this experience. And since people are highly motivated by money, I am thinking that these graduate students realize that when they have completed their master's degrees, they should be in a position to monetize their degree (their advanced level of business knowledge) and make more money. Essentially it is maximizing the return on investment.

OK – so those are my assumptions and expectations. However, I am continually shocked, surprised and disappointed when student work does NOT reflect a level of care. More shocked, more surprised when it is void of ANY care. I know, you want some examples right now. Here goes:

I am a teacher that believes in templates. I give my students templates for just about anything. Included in the templates are my detailed instructions for a great submission. I discuss format expectations, content expectations, grammar expectations, business brevity and conciseness expectations, and professional looking expectations. It is all there spelled out in black and white.

Yet – I am continually disappointed when all those expectations are clearly lacking. So I automatically assume that the student – does not care! Students – did my last statement register with you? In the absence of information that would obviously explain why there was such a lack of professionalism in their homework or assignment submission, I assume that you just don't care.

Now this may not sound like rocket science, but for some of you it may be a startling revelation. Why do teachers teach? If it is for the right reasons, the answer should be something like – they have a passion for the subject material and a passion for enlightening their students. 2nd question – what do teachers look for and appreciate completely? Students who want to learn and really care about what the professor is passionate about. That is what professors are looking for in the graduate student.

If I am like most professors, I will go out of my way for a student who cares about why I am teaching and what I am teaching. Let me share a recent example.

My daughter Amanda is currently a junior at University of Delaware. When she got her fall 2014 schedule, I was excited to see her taking accounting for the first time. I thought – wow, I can share my passion for my field of expertise.

Well after a few weeks, I found out why you can't teach your kids. They just don't want to listen and do what you suggest. Now, my friends had warned me. But I thought I could overcome the normal obstacles. No way!

So Plan B was for her to seek out assistance from the professor teaching the class during Accounting Lab time. I told my daughter that she should develop a relationship with her professor and let him know that she really cared for the subject. She took my advice. Yeah – one for the parents! Amanda also was under some academic pressure from me, her father. I told her that I was finished paying UD for "Cs." The next C she got was going to be on her dime, not mine. She quickly calculated the cost of a C to be $1,007 of UD tuition. At that moment, she was deeply motivated.

For the next 8 weeks (14 week semester), she and her friend Melanie went to Accounting Lab. They demonstrated to their professor that they cared about learning the material. They also showed him that they were willing to work hard to gain proficiency in the content.

At the end of the semester, Amanda walked out of her class with a great body of accounting knowledge. She had proven to her professor that it was important to her and that she was willing to work hard for a good grade. More importantly, when final grades were issued, Amanda received a B-. She was ecstatic. It was not a C.

Reflection Point ... in the Life Art Gallery

For all students: Really dig down deep and answer this question: why are you going to school? Why are you or your parents paying all this money to attend a university if you really don't care? So the next time you are required to submit an assignment to your professor – you might want to review this chapter in this book. Does the overall quality / and effort represent a source of caring?

One last story to savor. For the past year, I ask my students to read Ed de Bono's 6 Thinking Hats. They are required to read the book, which is an easy read, and then identify a current decision they are trying to make in their life with another party (to the decision). They get full credit when they have (1) read the book; and (2) applied the concept to a decision in their life.

Within the past year, I had this one student come up to me, right before he was to present to class, handed me his assignment, and told me that he had not finished the book, but took his best shot at completing the requirement.

My first thought was – why would you share with the class and me publicly that you did not complete the assignment requirements when everyone else had. And, furthermore, his assignment was clearly lacking the typical requirements of a graduate student.

I am sure he was motivated to lessen the negative impact on his grade. But all I remember thinking to myself was that – he just didn't care. BTW: he did not get a good grade in my class.

What do you see?

Victoria: Looks like some sort of brainstorming mind-map. I remember doing a lot of those mind-maps when I was in my bio-engineering program.

Michael: I agree. The center word could be short for introduction.

David: I like where you both are going. Perhaps it is how introductions should take place in the classroom.

The Importance of Intersection In the Introduction.

Once again, as a teacher, it is a small thing to do. However, when you are teaching 7-week blocks, you need to rapidly accelerate the formation of meaningful relationships.

I call this my "Introduction Template." Its primary purpose is give people a chance to get to know one another. Simple enough. But it has a secondary goal: to provide for intersections with people in the class.

Let's face it. It can be intimidating meeting people for the first time. Especially in class. Different cultures. Different age groups. Different socio-economic groups. Different degree concentrations all coming together for 7 weeks. 49 days. As a teacher, it is my responsibility to accelerate the meet-and-greet process as quickly as possible. After all, these students will need to depend on each other as they work through the class project and assignments with each other.

Before the first class, I complete the template for myself and post it on Discussion Board. The students get an opportunity to see the personal side of me.

I ask the students to complete their introductions before the first class as well. We are using time out of the classroom very effectively.

Week 1 (first class arrives). I make some references to several student introductions but we do not review them in detail (yet). There is a lot of "chemistry" that takes place in the first class.

During Week 2, I ask each student to come to the front of the class and informally present their bios to the class. This is such a great activity. Keep in mind that students have already had a chance to review and scan student profiles. At least enough where they can remember points of interest for future discussion.

Almost always, students discover "intersection points" with most of the students in the class. Whether it is parenting, hobbies, hometowns, musical affinities, or favorite foods – it provides a common intersection for relationships to form. Now this is a real investment of time. This can take between 1 and 1.5 hours in the classroom. But the investment in time is more than offset by relationships formed and the incremental ability to work together effectively and efficiently. Not to mention, there is generally a high feeling of respect that everyone appreciates and shows towards one another.

Reflection Point ... in the Life Art Gallery

All teachers should see the tremendous value of using a framework like this to accelerate the relationship building process in classrooms and online communities. What truly amazes me is how little it is done in the corporate world.

Now I have logged over 30 years in the corporate world and I cannot really recall a time when a senior leader took the time and effort to bring together a new team of people with this strategy in mind. The unwritten / unspoken words that generally prevail are --- you are all professionals. Find a way to compromise and work together because this project has to be completed. It usually has some ridiculous deadline that can't be achieved. The senior leader expects "corporate strangers" to figure a way of working without knowing each other?

We have all heard these immortal words, "The tone (or lack thereof) is set at the top." If results are priority, there will be no time dedicated to relationships. If relationships are a priority, there will be time dedicated to this important human activity.

Every senior leader has come to appreciate these timeless words, "You can pay me now, or pay me later." Every project operates under the same laws. Make the time upfront for relationship building – or you will spend lots of time on the backend, making up for the lack of relationships.

What do you see?

Victoria: Looks like alphabet soup.

Michael: Does it have something to do with a bass guitar rattling a door? You know bass notes and frequencies have very strong vibrations that travel through all walls and joists.

David: I would have to slightly agree with Michael. Since music was very important to my family, perhaps the bass guitar is a portal to something out of the ordinary.

Open Doors with an Ambassador.

Put people in the right Ambassador role and just watch the magic happen. Many colleges will leverage Ambassadors in their recruitment process. I remember when my oldest daughter Tiffany was considering Penn State because of their awesome meteorology program. My wife, Tiffany and I arrived on the very big campus of Penn State and were soon greeted by this highly extrovert junior named Lindsey. She was happy and very proud of her school. Before long we started to see Penn State through her eyes. As we were walking the campus, when she passed by students, she would cry out with great passion, "We are ..." And the reply that came back was a resounding "Penn State."

I knew before we left the campus that Mary (my wife) and Tiffany had already decided that Penn State was going to be the place that Tiffany would spend her next four years.

Tiffany graduated from the meteorology program and is currently a Meteorologist in Virginia Beach working in one of the big affiliates as their weekend weather expert. So, it was a great decision and investment in her career. But when I reflect on my first experience at "Happy Valley" -- I am always reminded that Lindsey had a significant impact on our decision to send Tiffany there – regardless of the fact that we had to pay out-of-state tuition for the next 4 years!

Back to the graduate classroom. When I started to teach multiple graduate courses, I started to re-visit the Ambassador program and how it could be leveraged in the classroom. By the end of the first class, I can pretty much tell who will struggle throughout the course and who will breeze through it. So after I had gathered some good data, after Week 2 (chapter quizzes, time spent in electronic learning modules, and homeworks) – I decided to nominate Ambassadors.

In Week 3 class, I could tell these people enjoyed the recognition and acknowledgment. More importantly, I explained to the Ambassadors that their primary role was to teach, inspire, and encourage (I call this the TIE concept) the other students. TIE the students to the course material and real world application.

I would now consider the "Ambassador strategy" as one of my rapid accelerators for learning and acquiring critical knowledge. Everyone always benefits when they can see and experience new content through the eyes of another.

Reflection Point ... in the Life Art Gallery

It doesn't matter if you are in the classroom or in the business world; almost any job requires the "active" dissemination of critical knowledge and information to the rest of the team. Identify your Ambassadors by function. Create a simple mission statement with the Top 3 Goals of the program. People love to be acknowledged for their expertise. Then just sit back and watch the magic happen.

Now go back and look at the artwork. Hopefully, you should see something that resembles –
I am an Ambassador!

What do you see?

Victoria: Looks like a really bad hair day. You know the kind of hair you get when the hair stylist over-dries your hair after the cut.

Michael: Looks like someone shot a bullet through an apple. But if you follow the trajectory of the bullet to the ground, we would assume that the shooter must be sitting on the ground.

David: The only stories I remember as kid that involved apples and trees were the William Tell story and the story of the forbidden apple in the Garden of Eden. If I have to choose, based on my Catholic upbringing, I am going with the Genesis story of original sin.

Leave the Forbidden Fruit on the Tree.

Business Ethics and the forbidden tree of knowledge. Fortunately, business ethics are being touched on (taught) in just about every business class. However, I am not sure how good the quality of discussions and exchanges are in the classroom between the students and the teacher.

I really like the parallel between "insider information" and the "forbidden tree of knowledge" that is obviously taken from Genesis, Chapter 2. As the story goes, both Adam and Eve taste the fruits of the forbidden tree of knowledge and immediately realize they have done something wrong.

While God does not put Adam and Eve in "orange suits", they are eternally banned from the Garden of Eden.

I get many miles from teaching on the insider information crime of Martha Stewart. Imagine being Martha Stewart and exchanging your personal integrity and ethics for a $40,000 trading profit --- despite being one of the most successful women in business.

I am not a football fan at all. Occasionally, I will watch some of the big games with family and friends. One of the little things that always amazes me is how the television networks can paint the digital line across the field indicating where the next 10 yards are for a first down.

I use that in my graduate class and explain that when someone approaches you and asks you to do something "unethical" – that a digital line does NOT appear on the floor they are standing on, indicating to them that they are not to cross. It would be cool –

but that technology does not yet exist for the enticement of an unethical act.

So we discuss that it comes down to the person to acquire sufficient knowledge of what is ethical and what is not. We even discuss the top 3 questions that one must ask themselves before they continue forward: (1) are there parties that will benefit and parties that will be harmed; (2) are there alternative courses of action that can be considered / pursued that will eliminate any party being harmed; and (3) if one continues forward, how will that story read if it is picked up on the front page of the local newspaper.

I share my life experiences at this point. I explain that I have been approached a number of times in my professional career to do something that I considered unethical or immoral. One of the best ways to diffuse a potentially awkward situation, especially if it is your boss asking you the question is to say this: "I am really sorry. I am uncomfortable with what you are asking me to do." At that point, the person on the other side of the conversation should have the smarts to immediately backtrack, rescind or drop it. The key buzzword is "uncomfortable."

Reflection Point ... in the Life Art Gallery

Try practicing saying that one line in the mirror. "I am very uncomfortable with what you are asking of me." It is not a matter of IF you will be approached; it is a matter of WHEN. And when that someone approaches you with request to bite into the "fruit of the forbidden tree" – now you should be able to flashback to the Garden of Eden and think – I know how this story ends. And it is NOT pretty.

What do you see?

Victoria: The person is a little creepy. Kind of reminds me of cactus-man being watched by an evil eye. The arm looks like it is going for this throat. Sorry. I guess I should not have watched another episode of the Bates Motel last night.

Michael: No, it reminds me of a puzzle that needs to be solved. I think it has something to do with body parts or limbs.

David: Wow, a blast from my childhood. There is no question about it. Looks exactly like Mr. Potato headpieces. You know, the facial pieces that allowed you to dress up a real potato.

The Fab 5 and the Learning Process.

I call them the Fab 5. The fabulous 5 senses that I think should be engaged in the learning process – as much as possible. So what are the 5 senses that I am talking about?

You should be able to guess most of them. Eyes, ears, mouth, the brain, and hands. OK – let's explore their critical roles in the learning process.

First, let's start with the eyes. Now, I believe we have two sets of eyes. Outer eyes and inner eyes. Everyone is familiar with the outer eyes – you know those 2 retina balls in our sockets. They are responsible for processing and seeing our environment. As a teacher, you should be constantly surveying the classroom environment. If you see eyes closing, due to fatigue or boredom (or both), or they are not fixated on you and the front of the classroom, then you should immediately do something! Something like asking that student what they think about what you just said. When I do this to my graduate students, they generally perk up, smile, and tell me that they have had a hard day. I fully understand. As an adjunct professor, I work during the day and teach at night. So, I completely understand. If there are two or more students' heads drooping, it is time for an exercise or break. I always tell my students that part of my teaching success comes from immediately adjusting to the collective awareness of the class.

The second set of eyes that must be acknowledged and engaged are what I call the inner eyes. No matter what I am teaching, I will often ask my students how this topic relates to the course "core." I go on to tell them that they must see, or create for themselves, a tentacle or relationship to the core – in their mind. For example, one of the courses I teach is Managerial Finance. This is a course about how to manage financial resources (primarily cash), and invest those monies prudently to generate a return for shareholders (owners). If I am teaching something on discounted cash flows – I make sure my students understand how this item relates to the core. It needs to be tentacled. Science has already determined that the brain best remembers information when it is paired to something else.

Next sense is the hands. I have already come to the conclusion that my graduate students, who use their hands continuously in the learning process, do extremely well. They take notes! The write down important things that I tell them to write down. This becomes the active part of learning process for the student. They must decide what to write down, and how fast to write it. When I am teaching an absolute critical piece of course content, I make sure that all my students are writing. I primarily do it to keep them engaged and alert – but please don't spill the beans why I do this!

The fourth sense is the ears. Sounds simple? Not really. There are so many things vying for our attention these days. So many things distracting us. Most of us honestly believe that we can do more work when we multi-task? Science has already proven that a "divided-mind" will compromise the quality of the tasks being performed. Now – let's assume that all my students are awake and listening. There really is a 2nd tier of listening. I call it "caring" listening. When you "care about" what you are listening to, it becomes much more of an active, engaging process. I believe when you are in this mode, you are "unconsciously" tuning out all other distractions. Think of the old rabbit ears that people use to locate on top of their TVs and manually adjust to get the best signal coming into their house. If you are listening with care, that is what you are doing. You are consciously adjusting your "antenna" to get maximum signal strength.

Now for the 5th and final sense, the mind. Sure, if you are doing all of the above, your mind must be engaged, must be processing, and must be working. However, I believe there is one more activity that you can do, to ensure maximum retention and absorption. I call it the "internalization" of the message.

It simply is not enough to just write down what the teacher says. That is good. But there is no guarantee that it will become part of your longer-term memory, which gives you the new skill and capability to really apply what you have learned. So I encourage my students, either in the class, or at home, to take what they have heard and written down, and write it in their own words. This is the process I call "owning it." Let me show you how I put this strategy into action as an adjunct professor.

When I am getting prepared to teach a new chapter in a new course, I will review all the teacher PowerPoint slides. One by one, I will review each slide, process the information, and develop what I call my Top 3 Notes. I actually write down these top 3 bullets in the Notes Section of the teacher slides. After I have completed this for all the slides, I now can say that I "own" the knowledge. In fact, many of my students have expressed to me that they appreciate my top 3 bullets more than the publisher's slide notes. But I do caution them, that they have to go through their own internalization process. Reading my notes does NOT make them own it. There are no shortcuts here.

Reflection Point ... in the Life Art Gallery

Now please go back to the Life-Art. Study the picture. As a graduate student, which senses are you engaging and which ones are you ignoring? Teachers, which senses are you engaging and which ones are you ignoring? Still not convinced? OK – let's have some fun with numbers.

According to my quick research on the Internet, the average lifetime earnings for people with a Bachelors and Master's degree is $1.8MM. The lifetime average for Associate degree holders is $1.1MM. The gap is $700,000. We now have our numerator.

Now let's estimate how many critical pieces of knowledge you are learning in undergrad/graduate school. Let's assume 12 three-credit courses for a Master's degree. And let's assume 10 chapters are covered in each course. Further, let's assume that there are 10 critical concepts in each chapter that will make you money. Or, in other words, 10 critical concepts that employers need to run a company. That would leave us with 1,200 critical concepts that earn people money. We have our denominator.

If we take $700,000 and divide it by 1,200 concepts, then we arrive at $583 per concept. So every time, as a student, if you miss the opportunity to truly learn, acquire and master a critical concept – you lose $583 of income. Do that 4 times, in 10 classes, and you have lost $23,320 in earnings. Or perhaps it is easier to think about giving up a brand new car to your co-worker. Why? Because they took learning a lot more seriously than you did in school.

The whole purpose of this Life Lesson is to make sure you are "creating" the kind of life that you want. Engage ALL the senses when learning something new. Hopefully, now you will think twice about writing that text in class.

What do you see?

Victoria: This can't get any simpler. It is just the word Excellence broken up. Not sure of its significance.

Michael: Maybe it is a motivational message that means to excel at anything in life, you have to be excellent at it.

David: Sounds kind of redundant, Michael. I think it has some connotation to the phase – to be excellent, one must go "above" and beyond.

When It Is Better to Know EXCEL Than to be Excel-lent.

It may not be witty. And you may have already guessed it. This section is dedicated to the Microsoft financial spreadsheet application called Excel.

As a graduate student, it is no longer possible to avoid learning and living without the excel worksheet. In my opinion, it is one of the greatest office / management tools ever created. It allows leaders, managers and analysts the ability to aggregate large quantities of data, formulate business models, and iterate many project assumptions before making a final decision.

Let me remind my readers that I am a CPA / MBA-Finance professional with more than 30 years of experience. Much of my work over my career has been working inside the Excel worksheet. So I am asking myself (right now) how many spreadsheets I have created in my life from scratch. I can conservatively estimate that I created at least 20 worksheets a week during my workweek. And as I got more proficient, I was comfortable applying and utilizing the tool at home. So by my rough calculations, I would estimate that I have created at least 30,000 spreadsheets in my life. No – the number seems too low. Let's bring that estimate up to 50,000!

Not convinced yet? Let me share a different angle. And this is what I share with my students if they start giving me pushback in the classroom when I talk about my love affair with Excel.

On the conservative side, let's assume that I have earned an average of $50,000 a year. $50,000 a year for 30 years that would put my life-to-date compensation (without bonuses and incentives) at $1,500,000. At least half of that income was generated as a result of me working in Excel. So this tool allowed me to generate $750,000 in gross earnings for my family. Not a bad ROI when you look at the cost and time to learn the basic functions of this incredible tool, right?

So what are the most critical functions of Excel that a graduate student should learn? Let me share a few practical scenarios that will answer this question.

When my students are close to completing my Managerial Finance class, I tell them that they should be able to do their own personal income taxes. So let me continue with this scenario.

As a graduate student, you should be able to build a spreadsheet that replicates your tax return. I know, some of you are now thinking, "What – that is what I go to H&R block for?" Well, if you can maintain an open mind right now, I can show you why this is a valuable opportunity to build good spreadsheet skills.

First, you should be able to record all your income with all of your deductions. Start with your gross income. Now you should be able to figure out what percentages are applied to your gross income to calculate your YTD deductions for your Social Security and Medicare. Keep going until you build formulas that can replicate the math logic to arrive at all those deductions. Pity – that we have all those deductions, right?

Once you have completed the income section, you are ready to record and aggregate your expenses deductions. Many of the deductions have ceilings so you will have to build that logic into the worksheet. You may have some challenges. But keep focused on the $750,000 that you too may be able to earn with and through this incredible financial tool.

You are not allowed to stop until you have replicated every number on your 1040 return and Schedule A. If you are self-employed, you will need to build spreadsheet logic for Schedule C.

Once you have completed this exercise, which by the way, is a great way to check and validate that H&R block did not make any mistakes, now you are ready to build your home/personal budget.

It amazes me how many people never even think of building a monthly financial budget. I tell my students that when you do, you immediately become conscious of your spending and saving at a whole new level. They don't believe me until they start their "Class Project."

Before I share my Class Project with you, let me share the genesis of how I created this amazing class project that truly provides a transformational learning experience for my students.

I worked with someone who decided to teach Accounting at a local university. Let's give him the name of Jim. Jim was an operations guy all of his life. While he could do Finance fairly well, he did not have the necessary credentials and qualifications to be teaching Accounting at all. You see, Jim had a good friend at this local university who provided Jim with an opportunity to explore the idea of teaching at the college level during the summer. I am assuming that the college administrator was thinking, "How much damage can my good friend Jim do to a few students during summer session?" Oh – those poor students!

Well Jim started teaching the course with a little bit more arrogance and cockiness than I thought was necessary. Each week he would share with me how easy it was teaching Accounting 101. I had my reservations, but things seemed to be going OK until he shared with me some of the early tests he was giving his students.

He shared with me some exam papers. He said, "Rich look – these students can't even figure out how to record a simple journal entry for the purchase of a parcel of land." While he only had 6 students in the class, they all seemed to be struggling on some basic concepts.

I immediately turned to Jim and asked, "What are you doing to bridge the knowledge of these students so that they can finally get it?" He said nothing. He went on to tell me that he just told his students to do more practice problems on their own time.

Pity. You see, Jim was teaching 21 and 22 year olds. I instinctively knew the problem that his students were having was that they could not "relate" these financial transactions to their personal lives. None of these students had ever had the opportunity to purchase a parcel of land. While I am not an expert in education development, between my personal journey with education, and raising and educating 4 kids, I was able to figure out that real learning, real long-term acquisition and retention of knowledge happens when you can "connect" it with things in their lives.

You will never believe what Jim shared with me several weeks before the class ended. After one particular class had ended, he walked out of the building with three of his students in front of him. He overheard one of them saying to the other two, "Jim is the worst professor I have ever, ever had. I wish I knew how bad it was going to get several weeks ago. I definitely would have dropped the class before the academic penalty would apply. Now I am going to fail, lose my money, and have nothing to show for my 15 weeks in class." At that moment, Jim did appear to be remorseful and dejected. His arrogance and cockiness had left him. All I could do was replay his statement of hubris in my head, "Rich, anyone in business can teach Accounting."

I share that real story with you because Jim was probably two years ahead of me as far as exploring the opportunity of teaching. But after Jim shared his revelation to me, I remember promising myself that when I would teach accounting in the future, I would create the most meaningful exercises to help them "connect" this body of knowledge to their own personal lives.

My experience with Jim happened in 2009. In 2011, I decided to go back and get my MBA in Finance. Why? I wanted to teach Accounting and Finance. And I wanted to teach at the graduate level. I wanted to prove my hypothesis – that leveraging personal life experiences to Accounting was the way to go!

I got my chance to teach my first graduate class in 2013. I remember how excited I was thinking about bringing 30 years of finance and accounting in the classroom. I remember receiving the syllabus for the class and thinking that it was now my opportunity to prove my theory.

After a week of racking my brain, I had my eureka moment. My flash of brilliance. Instead of doing what many teachers do in courses like these – which are the downloading of a company's financial statements, and then running a few ratios for the purpose of developing a financial analysis of the health of a company – I would leverage the journal entries of every student – through their checkbooks! What better way to teach accounting, journal entries, the general ledger, and the balance sheet and income statement – than to do it with their own personal financial transactions. It was a brilliant idea – if I say so.

So with my 30 years of Excel knowledge, I started building a financial template. With the help of some great friends at the time (Bryce and Ed), I was able to build a very robust template.

Here is the Class Project I use today in my accounting and finance classes. I ask my students to input every single transaction from their checkbook into the financial template. To do this, they are required to choose the correct "account" to debit and credit. Remember, they are recording transactions from their checkbook; so one side of the entry will always hit the Cash account. But they have to figure out whether they debit or credit the cash account. Then they complete the entry by selecting the proper account to hit. Might be Rent Expense or Dining/Recreation Expense or Health Insurance Expense.

Once they input their journal entry – remember this is their life, so they immediately understand the nature of the financial event – they go to the Income Statement and Balance Sheet and see how their journal entry posted. They rapidly learn the relationship of journal entries to general ledger accounts to financial statements.

The Class Project requires students to input 4 months of their lives into this financial template. Week by week, they are excited as they see what their financial lives look like through their very own Income Statement and Balance Sheet. I have used this exercise with over 200 graduate students so far. EVERY single student who experiences my Class Project tells me that it was truly an incredible learning experience for them – and for their significant partner! In fact, I have had many students ask me if I can build a template that would allow them to continue the project forever. I just smile and think, "How can I get this financial template in the hands of Intuit ☺"

You see, the reason why this works so beautifully is that I am connecting accounting to their personal lives. When they look at the Technology balance sheet account – they know exactly what item has been recorded to that account. TVs, iPad, iPhone, game systems, etc. They fully understand why we depreciate those technology items over 3 years. They now get obsolescence and the rationale for determining a useful life for each asset classification. I even have my students capitalizing their Clothing and depreciating it over 24 months. They picked the useful life of 2 years and they now understand that depreciation is simply recording (and estimating) how much of their economic resources were "used up" during the month. I never get tired at seeing their light bulbs come on in week 3 and week 4.

Reflection Point ... in the Life Art Gallery

Graduate students – now go back and look at the life art. Realize just how incredibly important this financial tool will be in your lives. Think about, dream and ponder just how much money, how much of your life-to-date compensation, can be generated through Excel.

And teachers – at the high school, undergraduate, and graduate level – remember this one phrase, "Make it Personal." When you can connect (I sometimes use the word tentacle) a new body of knowledge to something in their personal lives, they get it, appreciate it, and retain it. Perhaps, most importantly, they will enjoy it. There is nothing like seeing the facial expression of a student when they – remember, understand, and apply new knowledge!

What do you see?

Victoria: Very clever. I think it has something to do with project management.

Michael: Wow. You haven't come up with something that brilliant all day so far. But that is pretty good.

David: I see that the P character is supposed to represent some element of time. However, I am a little perplexed as to why there is a happy face on the M? But since I am Italian, I would have to say that I like the little happy guy.

Move over Gold. Time is the New Precious Commodity.

I should not have to cover time management in a book like this. But when I see how my graduate students treat their time, I realize we need another Life Lesson.

Would we all treat time differently if we had to go to the bank and withdraw 24 hours to live the next day? Perhaps. Here is our dilemma with time: if we waste it, nobody holds us accountable for it. The waste is not quantified. Nor is it ever recorded. We treat it like air. However, if we waste money, people will hold us accountable for it. The waste will get recorded. And likely hit someone's income statement.

I would say that about 50% of my graduate students have real problems and challenges with time management. They don't invest enough time to read the chapter content, they only scan it. They underestimate the amount of time needed to complete the homework assignments, and then get frustrated. They wait until the last minute to complete an online exam and then turn in the exam late.

I had this one very bright student recently turn in her midterm 3 minutes past the deadline. She would have gotten a 96 but instead received a lower grade due to her late penalty. When she approached me upset, she said to me, "Really – you are going to penalize me for 3 minutes?" I then asked her how long I gave the class to work on the exam. She said one week. I then asked her why she did not send me a note of explanation. She said she didn't know. Part of her issue was she really did not respect the deadlines I gave the class. The other reason was that she was terrible at project management.

Reflection Point ... in the Life Art Gallery

It doesn't matter if you are a student, teacher, manager, supervisor or worker. When you receive a new assignment, do you mentally assess what it will take to complete the task? Here is my proven strategy to manage your projects and time more efficiently and effectively: (1) Breakdown the assignment into 5 sub-tasks. (2) Estimate the time required to complete each sub-task. (3) Look at the due date. Now, working backwards put each sub task to a date on the calendar. (4) Start on the first sub-task as soon as possible. Fear of the unknown is the enemy of the procrastinator. Get over that fear quickly. (5) If you know you will need information and support from other people, schedule those things on the calendar too. Remember this is a discipline. It will not become a skill set unless you "apply it" several times. And when in doubt, reach out to a person in the know and ask them how long they think it should take to complete the task.

What do you see?

Victoria: OK – this one is not too hard. It is a picture of humble pie.

Michael: What does that term mean? Does it have something to do with humiliation and apologizing?

David: Yeah. It does. But once again, it lacks creativity. I think it needs a mountain of whip cream to be a little more visually stimulating.

Replace Hubris with Humility.

You're 33% Already There.

Humble Pie. This was the best artwork I could develop for Humility. Sorry. Onto the Life Lesson.

In some of my classes, I go through a quick exercise where I ask my students to list the endearing qualities of a great leader.

Humility is mentioned, but it usually appears at the bottom of the list.

Now, I ask my students to do the exercise in reverse. List those qualities that make for very bad leaders. What comes out on top are those qualities like dictator, arrogant, disrespectful, etc. All words which really represent the antithesis of Humility.

It is a strange paradox. We want humility most of all from other people. But yet we do not feel the need to give it. So, this is the Life Lesson I decide to bring into class. The pearls of parenting for almost 30 years.

I go on to explain to my students that after 29 years of parenting 4 kids (2 boys and 2 girls), I have come to this conclusion: The human soul hates to be told what to do. I share with them a parenting strategy that has served me well throughout the years. It is so good that my wife and I use it on each other. The funny thing is that we both know we are using it – we chuckle – but still are obedient to the request.

When my wife Mary was pregnant with Tiffany (our oldest) she attended some early development classes in our local community for first time mothers. Mary brought home some books. I started to scan one of them and came upon the ... Power of Choice.

The author went on to explain that when we offer our kids choices, two choices that we carefully structure, they respond well and pick the choice that best fits them. And this is where the magic happens – they pick their choice and become internally resolved to fulfill (complete) that action or commitment.

Even though most of my kids are grown, I still use this on my 15-year-old son. When I need to extract him from "Xbox land" – I will go into the basement and ask him this question: "Michael do you want to stop now or in 10 minutes?" He always chooses 10 minutes. But it is his choice. And he generally complies with his choice.

So if the human soul hates to be told what to do, what does it like, especially from a learning perspective? It likes the humility of one student asking another student for help.

My students quickly realize that if they are going to learn this material on schedule, they have to embrace, very early on, the ability to ask for help from another student. This is really hard for some students to do. I guess to some it is a sign of weakness and vulnerability. That is why I will utilize the Ambassador strategy with those students who are having difficulty reaching out for help.

By the way: If you haven't figured it out yet the reason why you are 33% there already when you replace Hubris with Humility are the letters "HU" from humility get overlaid on hubris. Hubris has 6 letters, hence the 33% already there.

Reflection Point ... in the Life Art Gallery

As a parent, there are no greater words for your kid to hear than, "Sorry Michael, I did not mean to snap at you." Or to say, "Amanda you are so good with pictures and technology. Do you think you can help me update my LinkedIn picture?" True story by the way!

If you are a student, embrace this Life Lesson quickly. Other students love to be validated for their knowledge and it opens up the portal for people to really enjoy helping you.

Business leaders keep in mind that "anti-humility" generally hits the top of the list of bad behaviors in managers and leaders.

So go have a slice of that humble pie.

And whip cream too.

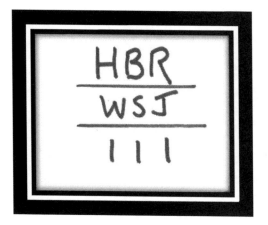

What do you see?

Victoria: HBR – isn't that something to do with human brain reaction analysis studies?

Michael: No, not sure about the HBR, but I know the WSJ stands for Wall Street Journal. Perhaps the 3 lines are pillars or supports holding up a sign for HBR and WSJ.

David: I think I am going to abstain from this one. It has no creativity at all.

Turn "On" Your Brain.

If you are going back to school to get your Master's Degree, please turn on your brain. At least turn on the portion that can make you lots of money.

Before I decided to write this section of the book, I wanted to make sure that my memory was serving me correctly – that is the universal sign for electricity being turned on is a line. So I walked into my music room (I am a classic rock drummer at heart) and looked over my buddy's guitar amplifier. (Of course it's a Marshall amp). Sure enough, the power switch had an O for the off position and a 1 for the on position. And boy when that amp is turned on, it gives the electric guitar all those sweet crunchy sounds. Enough of that.

HBR is Harvard Business Review. And WSJ is Wall Street Journal. While I am not getting any commissions from either one of those companies, I am strongly plugging for the reading and subscriptions for this magazine and newspaper. Especially since students are eligible for student discounts for both of them!

I am continually amazed when I find out that many of my students, who are sometimes in their 40s and 50s, do not read or even scan a financial newspaper or management journals. With each new class I teach, I explain to the students that when I was consulting, I literally used HBR's Daily Alert in some way, every day, in a meeting, phone conversation or project recap.

I go on and tell my students that it's like building a racecar and deciding to give it regular gasoline instead of nitrous oxide. When a student graduates with a Master's Degree, their total capacity for intellectual thought (hopefully) has been significantly increased. That means that it (the brain) is capable of more, better and faster critical thinking --- but you have to feed it fuel for thought. That is why I always gravitate to HBR especially. New practices and strategies along with recent failures are always being covered in HBR.

Reflection Point ... in the Life Art Gallery

Our job as teachers and professors is to build and develop critical thinking and capacity. Don't stop with your textbook and chapter slides. Encourage them to explore and stretch. HBR and WSJ are to the brain -- as nitrous oxide is to the racecar.

What do you see?

Victoria: It reminds me of the name Roy misspelled ☺

Michael: It probably has something to do with return on investment. I had this phenomenal Managerial Finance professor, Rich Savona, who taught me how to calculate the ROI on any investment. That is what I am going with.

David: I am thinking something like that too. Or maybe it could be that new hit show – Reality on Ice.

Move ROI from the Board Room To the Living Room.

ROI – Return on Investment. I know. If I am not careful, I will lose a number of readers and they will skip over this artwork for the next piece of art. My intention is not to get complicated. However, a simple understanding of ROI might help this reader from making a disastrous financial decision. Let's start with how this simple calculation works.

First, you calculate the "incremental" salary you will earn as a result of an undergraduate or graduate degree. You can take that over 20 years or 30 years. The incremental salary is your future cash inflows. Second, you estimate how much student debt you will accumulate to get your degree. This becomes your cash outflow.

Decide on an interest rate. You could simply use the cost of the loan. Drop into an excel spreadsheet and it will calculate the Net Present Value of the decision. If it is greater than 0, take the loans out. If it is not, do not borrow the money.

It's OK if you did not follow that exactly. Let's revisit some tried-and-true published guidelines: (1) Your total student debt should not exceed your first year starting salary or (2) your student debt payment should not exceed 10% of your pretax income.

Let's work through a simple example. Let's say that your son wants to be an Engineer and go to the University of Delaware. We do a little homework and find that 1st year starting salary for a civil engineer is about $50,000. If we consider Rule of Thumb #1 --- that means our son Ricky should not rack up school debt (total) more than $50,000. His actual school debt when he graduated (with his Master's degree) was about $45,000. He was clearly below the threshold.

Let's consider Rule of Thumb #2 – School debt payment cannot exceed 10% of your pretax income. Borrowing from the example above, 10% of $50,000 pretax salary is about $5000 or $416 monthly payment. If we take his $45,000 school debt at 6% for 20 years (240 months), we find that his monthly payment of $322 is clearly under the $416 threshold. Based upon this data and calculations, we would encourage Ricky to take the school loans.

However, on the other hand, I have learned that some students are carrying debt loads of $100,000 to $150,000 as they continue their master's degrees. What that means is that they must be able to qualify for a job with annual compensation of $100,000 (Rule of Thumb #1) or to get a job where the monthly pretax income of $7,164 or $86,000 using Rule of Thumb #2.

What I believe is needed is a complete financial grounding (awareness and understanding) with students before they sign on for any more student loans.

ROI, return on investment, must be brought out of the boardroom and into the living room. As teachers, we need to help students do this critical financial evaluation. Companies do this all the time. We need to make this a daily financial behavior for all graduate students.

Reflection Point ... in the Life Art Gallery

Ask your students if they have performed this critical financial evaluation. They are simple rules of thumb that can be intelligently applied. Make no mistake – my goal is not to discourage students from borrowing money to make a lifetime investment in themselves. On the contrary, my goal is to strongly encourage financial critical thinking on the relationship of the investment and the likely return (future job salary). Nothing against psychology majors, but there is no way that you can afford $100,000 of school debt with an entry-level psychology job. Perhaps you should re-consider that nursing or health administrative job. Now that conversation is worth its weight in gold!

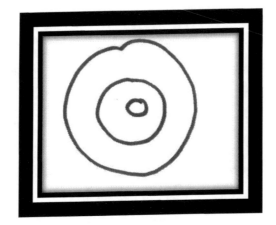

What do you see?

Victoria: Looks like a bulls-eye, a crappy one at that.

Michael: It reminds me of part of our solar system. Although much too round. Our solar system is highly elliptical.

David: Really. Looks like a sick or badly engineered flying saucer. Maybe a flying saucer that NASA took apart and then tried to rebuild. Ha, ha.

Every a Mighty Oak Has Many Rings.
Target the Important Rings.

The bulls-eye. It has been used by countless professionals to represent target markets, target customers, etc. So a book of Life Lessons that has tremendous business world application, should also have a bulls-eye piece of art. I would like it to represent the target markets of this book.

The center ring, the sweet spot of this book, is the Graduate Student. Why the graduate student? Because I have come to learn that many people (students) pursue their Master's Degrees with the wrong motivation.

I have met some students who honestly believe that the completion of their Master's Degree will magically and instantaneously open new doors of opportunity for them. Ironically, that is why I decided to bring my Life Lessons into the classroom to correct these silly notions and teach, inspire, and encourage.

Imagine this – I have had graduate students say to me, while they are working on their class project, that it was not important to regularly meet with and communicate with their team members. In fact, one person in particular, was so arrogant and disrespectful of their team members that when he was presenting his portion of his class project that he referred to his team as "them." I kid you not.

Now let's move on to the next ring. All the adjunct professors, teachers and administrative people whose job it is to … teach, inspire and encourage (TIE) graduate students to enroll and complete their degrees. It is critically important to pull in and incorporate Life Lessons to round out their academic training.

The 3rd ring now represents all the undergraduate students and undergraduate teachers and faculty members. While there are still tremendous applications of my Life Lessons in these circles, it really comes down to the passion of the teacher to share these experiences with students who might have limited life reference points.

The final ring, ironically perhaps the most important ring, are all the "real teachers" in the business world. I am referring to all the Supervisors, Managers, Directors, Vice Presidents, and Executive Leaders who have direct and indirect responsibility for people. Part of your job, whether you like it or not, is to TIE – that is to teach, inspire and encourage.

Do not limit your teachings to the one included in this book. If you reflect on the Artwork sufficiently, you should be able to identify your own Life Lessons. The important thing is that they be real, personal, and credible. Not to mention that they should naturally bring out your passion – as you mentally re-live the moment that you are teaching.

Yes, each one of these Life Lessons becomes, for me, an immediate re-living of the life lesson moment. That is why it works so well for me in the classroom. It is personal, real and credible.

Need more proof? OK – I will share a quick story of a lady who came into my life about two years ago. I met Pat in church one Sunday. You see, she had just been installed as the Executive Director of a local men's housing non-profit organization. Her job that Sunday was to create awareness of the men's shelter in the hopes that we would open our wallets and make a financial contribution.

To open our hearts (and wallets), she decided to identify a number of scripture readings that directly or indirectly supported her cause and our need to help. However, the delivery of her message became "robotic" – lacking the real passion and warmth that is generally needed to invoke donations.

I turned around to my wife in the pew and said – "I can tell that was so painful for her. I am going to reach out to her and help her improve the delivery of her message for the next church."

Well – I reached out to Pat for an introductory lunch. As I got to know Pat, I discovered that she was passionate about prison ministry and passionate about feeding the hungry and homeless. She started to come to life though her Life Lessons. At the end of our lunch meeting, I apologized for not making a financial donation and wrote her a check on the spot.

Reflection Point ... in the Life Art Gallery

The next time you are in the classroom, boardroom or conference room, when you are trying to TIE (teach inspire and encourage) – go to one of your many Life Moments that can become a Life Lesson.

What do you see?

Victoria: My dad was recently telling me a story about how a union worker refused to finish the job because everyone else would get mad at him. I think it is picture of union workers going to lunch.

Michael: No, it reminds me of the times when I had to change a course in my graduate schedule and when I needed help, no one seemed to be around.

David: I generally like to do what the crowd is doing. It is much more fun. Besides the finish line looks smaller and less inviting. I think those people are on their way to Grotto's Pizza on a Friday night in Newark Delaware.

Learn to Finish the Race. The First Time.

I know. It should be self-evident. It is. Or should I say the symptom is. What I am talking about is the general complacency I find in some of my graduate students when deciding to continue a course or drop it. Because some of my students are taking Finance and accounting for the first time, they often contemplate dropping the course after the 2nd week.

I can always tell on a student's face when they are pondering this question. After a few hours in the classroom, I can see the disengagement or disconnecting from the here and now. They carefully manage their eye contact. That is – they stop looking up at you in class. The final confirmation that I have lost a student is when they bury themselves in the safety and comfort of their iPhone.

Now there are some students who are legitimately on the fence. They either need a hit of oxygen (I jokingly say this) or they want me to proverbially walk them off the ledge – which I always do if a student is willing to do the work.

Some of my greatest accomplishments and success stories as an adjunct teacher are inspiring students to finish the race by overcoming their doubts and fears. Unfortunately, I have had students drop my class immediately when they find out that I expect them to work 10-15 hours outside of the classroom. It's their loss. Because I tell all my students that when they walk out of my classroom, they have legitimately learned a new life skill. They (now) have the ability to have a meaningful discussion with any CFO or controller of any company.

One of my greatest success stories was an older student who had little to no self-confidence. After Week 2, she approached me and said she was dropping. For all the wrong reasons. I immediately appointed an Ambassador for her. I asked her if she was willing to do the work and trust my program and class project. I got her to agree and hang in there.

When she completed her final and handed it to me, I could see she got a 100. She finished the class with a 96. 2nd highest student in the class. I walked her outside the classroom, as other students were still taking their final exam. She smiled at me and gave me a big hug. She thanked me for helping her complete the race and cross the finish line.

Reflection Point ... in the Life Art Gallery

There are students and workers all around us who have fears of doubt and self-confidence. Let's all keep in mind that we have all stumbled along the way and someone has either picked us up or carried us to the next station. You don't have to look far. Someone right now is in your field of vision (whether at work or in the classroom) who needs help finishing the race. Man up. Woman up. Change someone's destiny. Help them finish their race.

What do you see?

Victoria: My family owns a Chinese restaurant and I am helping them on the weekends all the time. Reminds me of the salt and pepper shakers that I have to clean on the tables.

Michael: Victoria, you have to be kidding. Being an engineer, I immediately see smokestacks. It has to be much closer to something like that.

David: The artist in me says that they are more like party hats. Not every item looks like a party hat. Only some of them. So I am going with 6 party hats.

Don't Get Caught in the Cold. Wear Your 6 Hats.

Six Thinking Hats, by Ed de Bono, gave me a powerful paradigm shift when it comes to communication and decision-making. I first learned about 6 Hats (for short) when I was consulting at a hospital in Pennsylvania. I just had come out of a meeting and one of the most talented managers there (Jay or

Jaybird as he would affectionately call himself sometimes), shared with me the essence of the book, which is a very quick read.

I immediately purchased my own copy and by the end of the week I had finished the book and had taken copious notes. I was getting ready to leverage this fresh approach to group decision making with my hospital client.

I recruited managers to "cogitate" on how it could best be used. I was starting to build excitement and expectations but unfortunately my consulting contract was closed out before I could truly demonstrate its power and effectiveness.

That was OK. I was already teaching at the graduate level. I had no problem bringing the book into the classroom and introduce it to my students. Now remember, I am teaching an advanced Managerial Finance class. They started to whine and ask why they needed to read a book like that.

So I started to connect the dots for them. I went on to explain that the most brilliant financial decision still has to be communicated, discussed, shared, and vetted with senior leaders in an organization. Some were skeptics. I went on to say that I never met a successful leader who was not powerful and effective in communication. On the contrary, I did meet many smart financial professionals who were clueless on the need to communicate effectively. Enough said.

The assignment I gave my students was this: summarize the book on a one page template I created for them, and then to apply the 6 Hats to a current (real-time) decision they were in the process of making. I then ask my students to present their decision in class and share how the 6 Hats helped them to make a better decision.

Every student, so far, has really "blown me away" or should I say exceeded my expectations. They take big personal decisions from their lives and put them under the 6 Hat microscope. Let me share some of the big time decisions they were all wrestling with: (1) whether to take a new job when their spouse was against it, (2) whether to buy a new home or rent a new apartment, (3) whether to still get married to their engaged partner (ooh – that was a close one), (4) whether to go on with their MBA program (that was a neat introspection), and (5) whether they should go to a family reunion – when the student had battled family dysfunction all her life. Wow! These were big, meaty life issues! And they all achieved a level of clarity that was provided to them by Ed de Bono's – 6 Thinking Hats!

Reflection Point ... in the Life Art Gallery

There have been so many books and textbooks on the topic of better decision-making, better communications, and better organizational leadership. Yet – they all seemed to lack a critical tool required to truly create and inspire a paradigm shift. Until now. Ed de Bono's 6 Thinking Hats is a seminal work that will slowly and quickly work its way into the American workplace.

If you are a student, go out and buy Ed's book. Then immediately apply to a current decision you are trying to make. If you are a teacher, go out, buy the book and consider adding it to your course materials. The only way better decision making happens is when we better understand each other's position more effectively.

And if you occupy one of those managerial and leadership titles, and are tired of the infighting and backstabbing, well go out and buy a few hundred copies of this book. Require its reading. Now require all your teams to apply it to the current project / decision / dilemma they are all struggling with. You will be amazed at how it can diffuse very unhealthy and stressful infighting.

Just don't forget to celebrate when you achieve a new level of success. All you need to do is to go out and buy some good cake. The team is already wearing their "party hats." ☺

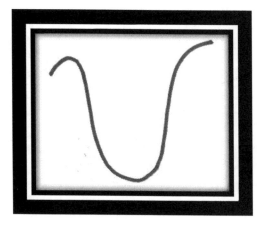

What do you see?

Victoria: My grandmother was big into sewing. I would watch her thread that small little needle eye all the time. I was amazed at how fast she did it. So, it reminds me of a strand of thread. Maybe it has something to do with the importance of threading certain competencies throughout the MBA program.

Michael: I am impressed Victoria. That is probably the first time you have taken this assignment seriously. Rich would be impressed with your insight. However, for me, it looks more like a valley and hill. Maybe it has something to do with gaining momentum during our education journey.

David: Both of you are being way too logical. I think it may have something to do with the Larger Circle that we explored before. Maybe we all start with a single line and then figure out how to build a community of people. Perhaps, it is our job to connect both sides to form the circle.

Every Class Has Its Dip. Plan to Get On the Other Side.

The Dip by Seth Godin. One of the smallest and most thought provocative books I have read in the past 10 years. As adjunct professors, we should highly recommend this book to our graduate students.

Simply put, Seth Godin teaches us that everything in life has a "dip". Now really study the life-art. Every new activity, every new subject to be learned, starts out with excitement and potential. The X-axis represents the total time to learn and master anything in life. The Y-axis represents, in my mind, a combination of excitement, enthusiasm and success – in learning something new. Let me highlight a new activity in my life right now – learning the guitar.

First, let me remind you that I am a classic rock drummer for the past 40 years. Drumming is my passion. However, I have always wanted to learn the guitar as a secondary instrument. After playing in front of audiences for many years, I am somewhat envious of the guys with the guitars who get to stand in front and get all the fame and glory. They get to experience the fans. What I get to see and experience --- only the butts of the guitarists who are in front of me. Oops – sorry for that digression.

OK – so I started my journey with the guitar about 9 months ago. There was excitement and great anticipation as I cleaned up my beautiful acoustic guitar and started to go out and buy new accessories, new guitar strings, etc.

I dug out all my guitar chord books to give me a quick reference when I needed to remember how to form a particular chord. You see, my new motivation was that my 15-year-old son was learning how to play the guitar and I wanted to be a good role model. I was getting ready for him to say things like: "this is too boring, my fingers hurt, I have more homework to do, and I can't even play one song yet." I figured that the best way to help my son overcome these issues was to say to him that I completely understood. I was experiencing the same thing.

Well after a few weeks, I started to experience the downside of the dip. This is the part when my fingers started to hurt and callous up. This was the part where my wrist would get frozen because I was playing a chord too long.

As the weeks go by, I continue to slide down the dip. I am practicing every day but not seeing any real progress. When I look to validation from my wife Mary, and ask her if she hears any progress, she says, "go back to your drums." (OK – she didn't really say that. I embellished the comment for effect :-)

But I slug on. And then one day, it happens. I am able to slide up and down on the fret board where the chords I have been playing for months now sound like a song. A real song! It was the validation I was looking for. This is how the dip works in life, especially the business world. It completely weeds out (eliminates) all the people who are not serious about learning.

We see the dip play out all the time. Think about all the people who make New Year's resolutions and join a fitness club. Memberships swell in January and February. As March comes around, fitness club memberships level off (again). All the people who quit found out how hard it is to stick with something that requires real commitment and work.

So how does the Dip really play into graduate school? Because students need to know that every class has its dip. There will be late night homeworks to complete and submit on time. There will be arduous class projects that need to be managed across several students who you may or may not know. There will be midterms and finals that need to be studied for. However, the spoils and acknowledgments are there. They are on the other side of the dip.

Reflection Point ... in the Life Art Gallery

If you are a graduate student, be honest with yourself and your family. There will be work. There will be concepts that are hard to learn and even harder to study for. But the dip is your friend. You know that there will be lots of people who start and never finish. There will be more people who finish and are willing to accept a C. However, you are determined to leverage the power of the dip and get your A+. An A says that you slugged through the dip and came out on the other side. These are the spoils that make a difference in life.

If you are a teacher, please prepare your students for the dip. Not to scare them, but to encourage them and support them. It's a little bit like running a marathon. They need to know what mile marker they are at. Perhaps more importantly, as teachers we must understand the kind of motivation and support each mile marker needs. I know when my students are running out of gas in my courses, when they are close to the finish line, and when they know they need to start sprinting to get through the final, I become the cheerleader they need. Wow – what a feeling and sense of accomplishment to see that student, who was about to drop out of the class, cross the finish line with that A or B!

THE END (of this book, not the journey)

Made in the USA
Middletown, DE
08 August 2015